Saving America and Other Plays

by Ludmilla Bollow

A Samuel French Acting Edition

New York Hollywood London Toronto

SAMUELFRENCH.COM

Copyright © 2009 by Ludmilla Bollow

ALL RIGHTS RESERVED

CAUTION: Professionals and amateurs are hereby warned that *SAVING AMERICA AND OTHER PLAYS* is subject to a Licensing Fee. It is fully protected under the copyright laws of the United States of America, the British Commonwealth, including Canada, and all other countries of the Copyright Union. All rights, including professional, amateur, motion picture, recitation, lecturing, public reading, radio broadcasting, television and the rights of translation into foreign languages are strictly reserved. In its present form the play is dedicated to the reading public only.

The amateur live stage performance rights to *SAVING AMERICA AND OTHER PLAYS* are controlled exclusively by Samuel French, Inc., and licensing arrangements and performance licenses must be secured well in advance of presentation. PLEASE NOTE that amateur Licensing Fees are set upon application in accordance with your producing circumstances. When applying for a licensing quotation and a performance license please give us the number of performances intended, dates of production, your seating capacity and admission fee. Licensing Fees are payable one week before the opening performance of the play to Samuel French, Inc., at 45 W. 25th Street, New York, NY 10010.

Licensing Fee of the required amount must be paid whether the play is presented for charity or gain and whether or not admission is charged.

Stock licensing fees quoted upon application to Samuel French, Inc.

For all other rights than those stipulated above, apply to: Samuel French, Inc. 45 West 25th Street, New York, NY 10010.

Particular emphasis is laid on the question of amateur or professional readings, permission and terms for which must be secured in writing from Samuel French, Inc.

Copying from this book in whole or in part is strictly forbidden by law, and the right of performance is not transferable.

Whenever the play is produced the following notice must appear on all programs, printing and advertising for the play: "Produced by special arrangement with Samuel French, Inc."

Due authorship credit must be given on all programs, printing and advertising for the play.

ISBN 978-0-573-69727-2   Printed in U.S.A.   #29156

No one shall commit or authorize any act or omission by which the copyright of, or the right to copyright, this play may be impaired.

No one shall make any changes in this play for the purpose of production.

Publication of this play does not imply availability for performance. Both amateurs and professionals considering a production are strongly advised in their own interests to apply to Samuel French, Inc., for written permission before starting rehearsals, advertising, or booking a theatre.

No part of this book may be reproduced, stored in a retrieval system, or transmitted in any form, by any means, now known or yet to be invented, including mechanical, electronic, photocopying, recording, videotaping, or otherwise, without the prior written permission of the publisher.

IMPORTANT BILLING AND CREDIT REQUIREMENTS

All producers of *SAVING AMERICA AND OTHER PLAYS* must give credit to the Author of the Play in all programs distributed in connection with performances of the Play, and in all instances in which the title of the Play appears for the purposes of advertising, publicizing or otherwise exploiting the Play and/or a production. The name of the Author *must* appear on a separate line on which no other name appears, immediately following the title and *must* appear in size of type not less than fifty percent of the size of the title type.

TABLE OF CONTENTS

Saving America 7
Flickering Fireflies 21
The Beach Club 35
Shelter Skelter 71

SAVING AMERICA
(A Play in Ten Minutes)

The premiere performance of **SAVING AMERICA** was on October 29, 2005, at the Ohio State University Department of Theatre in Columbus, Ohio. The cast was as follows:

MARTHA..Nancy Buehler
REGINA...Gloria Krause
GEORGE..Bob Krause
JASPER...Allan Munro

CHARACTERS

MARTHA – Homeless woman.

REGINA – Synthetic attractiveness. Apparent facelifts, injected beauty treatments. Upscale attire.

GEORGE – A soft spoken poet in earth tone clothing.

JASPER – Muscular, but fading. Some hint of cowboy attire, possibly fringed vest. Western accent. Constantly moving or pacing.

VOICE – Sometimes Male, or Female, or Group. Not always projected from same area. Mechanical, cold sounding, almost rote.

(*SETTING:* Bare stage. Five metal chairs lined across the back.)

(*TIME:* Not discernable.)

(*AT CURTAIN RISE:* Each enters from left, holding white envelope. Last is **MARTHA**, somewhat confused. Harsh sound of metal door clanging shut.)

MALE VOICE. *(Tone. Introductory vibration sound.)*
Attention! We will begin. It is important to keep to schedule. We want to assure you, everything will be carried out in your best interests. Further instructions will follow. *(Tone.)*

REGINA. Ridiculous! Utterly ridiculous!

JASPER. How long you s'pose they gonna keep us?

REGINA. There is no legitimate reason why I was ordered to come here.

GEORGE. I was in the midst of this euphoric poem. Waiting for the words to descend –

MARTHA. Some guy, just handed me this letter, right on the street.

JASPER. Sure looked pretty official. "Open immediately!"

GEORGE. Everything about it – cold. Impersonal words. Composed by a machine.

REGINA. "Be prepared to take a journey. Bring nothing along." What kind of preposterous –

MARTHA. Jerked my bag right out of my hands, before I could enter. Geez.

REGINA. My expensive jewelry – confiscated. My diamond watch –

JASPER. You don't think they would have carried it out, imprison us, if we didn't all show up?

REGINA. "Please report at 10 a.m. sharp!" Whatever for?

GEORGE. It projected such an urgency. I avoid urgencies, except when a poem demands it.

JASPER. *(Begins flexing and exercising.)* Keep myself limbered up. Why I'm in such good shape.

(Looks up toward possible speaker)

Hope I'm not breakin any of your rules.

REGINA. I was due at my doctor's office today. Now I don't know when I can get another appointment.

MARTHA. You sick or something?

REGINA. Do I look sick to you?

MARTHA. Lost my glasses, things look mostly blurry.

REGINA. I'll sue whoever's responsible. My last surgery could be utterly ruined, if –

(Outlines facial area with probing fingers.)

MARTHA. *(walks about)* Anybody got extra food? Didn't find no throw away eats today *(beat)* or yesterday.

JASPER. Didn't you read the letter? "Do NOT bring anything with you!"

MARTHA. Got nothing to bring… So, maybe I'll go out, see what I can find.

GEORGE. The doors are locked. I can feel – that locked in sensation.

REGINA. Why don't they just get on with it. Tell us – something.

JASPER. You know, this could be one of those reality TV shows. Go through all kinds of wacky stuff, and then – "Surprise!"

GEORGE. I don't think so. But, it does feel – unreal.

JASPER. Those reality shows, I tell you, they are unrealer than real.

GEORGE. Why only four of us? Why five chairs? What's our connection?

REGINA. None. None whatsoever. *(pause)* Water? Anybody see any water about? I need to keep from dehydrating.

MARTHA. Probably no bathroom either. Huh, used to that.

GEORGE. Something – the connection – Must be our age. We're probably all over eighty.

REGINA. I'm nowhere near eighty.

JASPER. I never give out my age, so how –

GEORGE. Social security. Somehow they have your age.

JASPER. Well, maybe –

GEORGE. Ways to get all our information. Computers have it all.

MARTHA. I don't remember applying. Still, I get checks, at the station, when I go there.

MALE VOICE. *(Tone.)* You will sit down now. Listen carefully. The Group thought it would be easier to tell you the plan, after you arrived. Printed letters can get to newspapers, the Internet. Be assured your letters are programmed to disintegrate in a very short time.... You were chosen to be part of a new experiment, *(beat)* to make the last days of your life easier, *(beat)* to save America! We have found the solution that is best – for everybody.

FEMALE VOICE. Be assured, you will be treated humanely. Your names will be recorded in a special book, and some day the world will know of your willing sacrifice – to save America. We will speak to you again shortly. *(Tone.)*

MARTHA. Save America? Not interested. Just saving myself.

REGINA. I won't be part of any mass medical experiment. This is not for me!

JASPER. Record our names? Hell, mine's already recorded – rodeo records, horse roping –

GEORGE. They're not telling us everything. Something they're not revealing – yet.

MARTHA. Ever try to get information from government places? Mush mouths, all of them.

REGINA. So, what are we supposed to do now?

GEORGE. Nothing. I don't think there is anything we can do. It's too late. They've already decided.

(Lights out and up. Everyone is more tired and weary.)

JASPER. Two hours we been here. Why?

REGINA. It has to be a joke. A very sick joke.

MARTHA. *(huddled in corner)* Wake me up, if you hear anything. Or food comes along.

GEORGE. *(waking up)* I heard far away words in my dreams – But, couldn't make them out.

MALE VOICE. *(Tone.)* Thank you for waiting. Since this is our first group, we are still working things out as we go along. We know you have questions. We hope our explanation will be a sufficient answer. Please sit, and listen carefully.

FEMALE VOICE. We are a new government agency, all information strictly classified, called "Saving America". As you all know, the country is steadily being drained of all of its finances. Economy is irreparable. There is no way to increase tax funds. Why? Because of the astronomical rising medical costs. We have done much research, and the greatest financial experts, at secret summit meetings, have come up with a solution that would be fair to all.

GROUP VOICE. – We do not want to ration health care.

– We can no longer raise taxes, without an open rebellion.

– There is nowhere else to get additional funds. Other countries are suffering also.

– Our hospitals are being choked, health care degenerating into chaos.

– No other solutions have helped. Abortion. Birth control. Locking our borders.

Our resources will be gone shortly if we don't take drastic preventative measures.

MALE VOICE. This is the plan The Group came up with. We are still refining many things. So, please bear with us. Consider yourselves heroes of our country, the same as your founding fathers were. Willing to sacrifice themselves for the well being of others. Your children. Your grandchildren. *(beat)* We will be back shortly. *(Tone.)*

(All are quiet for a few moments.)

MARTHA. *(rising)* How the hell can we save America? Waay too late!

JASPER. *(rising)* I'm not going along with this. No way. Gotta figure some plan to get outta of here. These muscles, they're still strong –

GEORGE. Authorities are stronger. It's they who have the power.

REGINA. I'm not interested in saving America. Whatever gave them that idea?

(Tears up letter with great deliberation.)

JASPER. An experiment? Maybe they have a new drug – to make us younger.

REGINA. *(Pauses in tearing.)* I might consider that.

MARTHA. I'd consider anything to put in my mouth right now.

GEORGE. Have you ever seen cattle herded into pens – waiting to go to slaughter houses. They have no idea what is going to happen to them. No idea at all.

REGINA. We're human. We're not cattle.

JASPER. We got rights.

MARTHA. Don't have money, got no rights.

REGINA. I have ample funds. Top lawyers.

GEORGE. Do we give up? Do we fight? Does it matter?

MARTHA. Course it matters. Whatever happens to us matters.

(Lights out and up. All are seated. During following each does something to destroy letter as they hear certain things.)

MALE VOICE. *(Tone.)* Sorry to keep you waiting. We had to prepare carefully – how to tell you. Go over it all once more. Following is our proclamation for Saving America!

FEMALE VOICE. We have decided that what is killing America – is the old people. Because of all the advances in medicines and health care, we have an excess of old people, and we don't know what to do with them anymore, humanely. Thus, we decided to start with those eighty years of age. That will save our social security benefits from imploding, hospital and hospice care from collapsing, medicare payments going beyond repair. The statistics have all been figured out – to everyone's benefit.

MALE VOICE. The problem – what to do with excess eighty year olds? How to humanely let them go, without uproars from political groups, religious sects. If our plans went public, they would try to stop us. But, because this is a secret government program, no one will ever find out. There will be no bodies to discover –

JASPER. Now, just one minute there –

MALE VOICE. Listen carefully! You will no longer have a say in the matter.

FEMALE VOICE. You will be our human guinea pigs. We have already experimented with animals. The method is painless. There will be no evidence left, anywhere. Our biggest problem will be in the gathering of the elderly. We will solve that shortly. Also, the aftermath when it is realized they have disappeared. However, by eighty, there are few connecting ties, so few that care, that will even bother to question. We are counting on this.

MALE VOICE. At first we were not going to reveal what was going to take place – and you would never know. Then, we decided you deserved to know what is going to happen, give you time to prepare, however each of you would like to spend your final last hour. There will no longer be any contact with anyone outside of this room. These metal rooms are moveable, and will not be in the same place twice. Just a simple trailer room. Soon these gray boxes will appear all across America. In one place, then another, non-traceable. And we – we are just voices – no way to track us either. No other humans are in this trailer, only you.

FEMALE VOICE. The most painless, bloodless, non-traceable way to remove you from the face of the earth, and to keep everyone equal – There is no discrimination for race, gender or religion, only age. You have already led a good life. The government has taken care of you throughout all these years. Now is the time for you to give back, to the next generation.

GROUP VOICE. You will have one final hour, to consider all we have told you. To make any conclusive preparations, religious reconciliations. The method we have chosen –

MALE VOICE. We have perfected a vaporizing machine. Within one minute or less, you will be vaporized from the face of the earth. Nothing will remain – only what you did in the past, recorded or remembered elsewhere.

GROUP VOICE. Once our goals are met, the economic situation stabilized, we plan to raise our age criteria to ninety. We don't know yet. As we said, this is an experiment. Just as Social Security was, the Welfare System – a new government program to help those most in need of help.

FEMALE VOICE. As part of your final preparations, we have laid out a special banquet in the next room, The Termination Room. You will be given one hour to partake of a grand array of food.

MALE VOICE. But, before you go to the Termination Room, we would like one last statement from each of you. Some expression regarding what you have just heard. We want to know what people will say, knowing they are entering their last hour on earth. This will help us in our future preparations. Your words will be recorded, for possible further study.

GROUP VOICE. After you have said your words – take your time, you will then file out, the door to your right. *(Tone.)*

MARTHA. Food? All I can eat? I don't care what happens to me after that. I can dream I died and went to heaven. One last good meal! Then nothing else matters.

(Exits right. Tone strikes once.)

JASPER. It's a joke. I know it's one big heapin joke. Okay. Gonna find out for myself, right now. Settle it once and for all. There is no way in hell they can do what they said they would do. No way!

(Singing as he leaves [Streets of Laredo].)

"Oh, beat the drums slowly and play the fife lowly,

Take me to the green valley and lay the sod o'er me –

For I'm an old cowboy and I know I done wrong... ."

(Tone strikes twice.)

REGINA. *(still pacing)* I didn't sacrifice all these years, go through all the numerous tortures to keep myself looking young, to have it end this way. The exercises, vitamins, operation after operation. Age does not have to go forward, age does not have to qualify what happens to us... . Age is only how you feel. Age is not a number. Eighty is not some cut off –

(Sits in chair an begins to cry. Stops.)

And now my makeup will be all ruined. I don't want to go out looking old and ugly – without makeup. This isn't how I wanted to leave the world. I planned to be here much longer –

(Bewildered pause.)

What they said? The body would be vaporized? That would mean, no further decay. No rotting in a grave. No endless clawing and fighting to maintain the perfect figure, erasure of wrinkles, smoothing the skin, reducing the fat, perfecting the lines. *(pause)* I'm tired of the struggle. There would never be an end to it. Never. *(stands)* I shall go, but that does not mean that I ever gave up.

(Exits right. Tone strikes three times.)

GEORGE. *(Looks about.)* I wish I could write some words for you. Memorable words. But, what are words? Just alphabets mixed up on paper? It's the emotions that count. But, my heart can't feel right now, it's locked in too. Without feeling. I can express – nothing.

(Looks at empty chair.)

Are you the lucky one? The one who didn't accept the summons? The escapee who won't know when your time has ended? You, who have managed to retain more than the allotted hour – or have you just gathered more time? *(beat)*

Last words? None of my own, but someone else's reverberates. Hope I can remember – it's been so long… .

(As he exits.)

"I regret – that I have but one life – *(beat)* – to give for my country."

(Multiple Tones, then clang of door shutting as lights dim.)

The End

PRODUCTION NOTES

MARTHA – Wears baggy, shoddy clothing.
REGINA – Wears expensive, high label attire.
GEORGE – Combination of soft flowing earth tone clothing.
JASPER – Hint of cowboy attire, possibly fringed vest, fancy boots.

Note: None wear hats, jewelry, or watches.
   Each carries a business sized white envelope.

FLICKERING FIREFLIES
(A Play in Ten Minutes)

The premiere performance of **FLICKERING FIREFLIES** was held at the Secret Rose Theatre in the NoHo Arts District, California, and was produced by Fire Rose Productions on December 3, 2004. The cast was as follows:

SHOO..Mimi Chen
BUZZ...Rollence Patugan
LUNY..Rebecca Riker
MOONY..Ned Kletz

CHARACTERS

SHOO FLY – Mother. Overly soothing motherly voice. (Name is pronounced elongated "Shooooo Fly")

BUZZ FLY – Father. Deep ponderous voice. (Name is pronounced elongated "Buzzzzz Fly")

LUNY FLY – Teenage female. High pitched, maybe even squeaky voice. Always flitting about, gyrating dances, flapping her wings flirtatiously.

MOONY FLY – Teenage male. Stomps about. Flexes muscles.

(*TIME*: Today)

(*PLACE*: Anywhere)

(*CURTAIN RISE*: Complete darkness. One by one, tiny greenish lights begin to glow and blink in the background. Then we hear, giddy chipmunk-like voices. [More voices can be added, or pre-recorded, to make it sound like a huge gathering.]

VOICE. Now, let's all sing our theme song for Firefly Fest! One more time!

ALL. (*to tune of "Twinkle, Twinkle, Little Star"*)

"Flicker, flicker, little fly – Meet and mate and multiply! When the day begins to dark – Comes the time we show our spark!

Flicker, flicker, little fly – Meet and mate and multiply!"

(*Giggling, laughing. Then separately, four tiny flashlights move forward, blinking on and off. Scene brightens as other lights dim.* **LUNY** *and* **MOONY** *are flitting about. Parents are perched either end of huge log.*)

BUZZ. All right children, Luny and Moony, just settle down now.

LUNY. Can't. Just can't! Been waiting forever for this night, to finally flitter and fly!

MOONY. I'm itching so mightily to bust loose. Zoom out of here! And be on my own!

BUZZ. Welll, before you "bust loose," and go out on your own –

SHOO. – To your very first mating party –

BUZZ. Your mother, Shoooo Fly, and I need to talk to you, about –

LUNY. Hurry, will you please! Ever since I was a little glow worm, I've dreamed of this night. Blinking for my mate, and –

SHOO. Yes, Luny, we know it's an exciting time of your cycle for you. Bursting into womanhood.

MOONY. And manhood!

SHOO. But first, we, as responsible parents, need to give you – ah, mating instructions. Righttt Buzzzz Fly?

BUZZ. Righttt, Shoooo Fly!

SHOO. You two need to know about –

SHOO & BUZZ. Safe mating!

LUNY & MOONY. Bug off, will you guys. We know all that stuff already.

MOONY. Birds and bees –

LUNY. And watch out for fleas, and all that disease.

(**SHOO** *opens picnic basket, spreads cloth and items on log.*)

BUZZ. Oookay, we'll take a short break then. Shoooo Fly has packed a nice picnic basket for us.

SHOO. Earthworm sandwiches, pickled snails, dried slugs and –

MOONY. Can't I just take my grub and chomp it along the way?

LUNY. I'm too excited to eat. All I did as a larvae was munch and munch. I'm ready for some blinking action. Now!

SHOO. It'll be a long night, for all of us. So, let's just have some family time. Come on, sit, just for one minute. It's all fast food.

(**CHILDREN** *sit reluctantly and all begin eating.*)

BUZZ. *(clears throat)* Now that we have your attention. It's time to tell you – The basics of mating –

SHOO. You see, the male flies and flashes –

MOONY. I can do that.

BUZZ. And the female lies in the brush or grass, and flashes back.

LUNY. I'm ready to lie!

BUZZ. *(rapid and rote)* Now then, fireflies contain special cells in their abdomen that make a light. The cells contain a chemical called lucifern and make an enzyme called lucifrone. The wavelength of light given off is between 510 and 670 nanometers –

LUNY. Stop already, with the lectures! We learned all that at Fly High.

MOONY. And we're ready to do it!

LUNY. I don't want to use up my glow, just sitting on a log.

MOONY. My luminous testosterone is growing and glowing!

LUNY. My lucifern hormones are hot to light up and flash for my blinking mate!

BUZZ. But, this is our last chance to instruct you –

SHOO. Luny, after you lay your first 500 eggs – *(sniff)* Well, I won't be around to help, advise you anymore.

MOONY. You mean there's 500 kids, first time round!

BUZZ. Guess they didn't want you to know that at Fly High, did they? Just the fun stuff.

SHOO. We must also warn you – about – the false flies!

BUZZ. Who hang out in certain muddy, sleazy, off-limits places.

SHOO. A whole different breed, than we are. They use aggressive mimicry, and falsely imitate the "femme fatale firefly."

BUZZ. And once the male is lured –

SHOO. The femme fatale fly –

BUZZ. Pounces on the male –

SHOO. And eats him!

MOONY. Dad, you already told us this stuff. Old age? Memory slipping?

SHOO. Well, just remember to stay away from those public parks too!

BUZZ. Dangerous!

SHOO. The sprayers!

LUNY & MOONY. *(mimicking in terror)* Ooooh! The sprayers!

SHOO. Nothing to make fun of.

BUZZ. If those poisonous toxins ever hit you – it's Bye Bye, American Fly!

SHOO. They're supposed to be spraying for mosquitoes only, but –

BUZZ. Those homosapiens cannot tell the difference. All bugs look alike to them.

MOONY. Mom and dad, they only spray the parks in the daytime.

LUNY. They told us that. At Glow Camp.

SHOO. Doesn't hurt to be told again. And make sure you keep away from those perverted strangers. Who want to lure you –

BUZZ. *(Scary voice.)* Into their jars!

MOONY. No way! Nobody's putting me in a jar!

LUNY. I can fly so fast with these new wings, nobody will catch me, except, maybe a manly male fly.

MOONY. Can we go now, light up the sky?

SHOO. No camp songs around the old log? Just one more time?

MOONY. Nah! We hate singing – not our style. We'd rather be blinking.

BUZZ. What about a farewell toast then? Now that you're old enough.

SHOO. We saved a whole bottle of Wild Juniper Juice. Just for this occasion.

BUZZ. Makes you forget all your troubles....

MOONY. Nah, we're not into drinking home brew either. Makes our diving too zig zaggy.

LUNY. So, can we log off now? Go flying on our own?

BUZZ. Okay. Permission granted. Go, seek your fortunes, whatever they might be.

SHOO. Farewell my pets. Go gently into this good night.

LUNY & MOONY. *(As they leave. Repeating in same tone.)*
Good night. Good night. Good night.

SHOO. We tried our best, to prepare them.

BUZZ. Yes we did. *(beat)* And now, our final, last few hours –

SHOO. Don't talk about it! Let's act as if we still have forever.

BUZZ. Well then, how's about finishing the last of the Juniper Juice?

SHOO. I thought you'd never ask.

(They pass the bottle back and forth, schlurping noisily.)

BUZZ. Still potent stuff.

SHOO. Oooh. Good to the last drop! Makes me feel – Well, my hormones aren't as dead as I thought they were.

(Snuggles up to him.)

BUZZ. I can't fly too well when I drink. And my flickers get a little too woozy. But the old testosterone, it's still blinking. Not as bright as it used to be, but –

SHOO. Good enough for me.

BUZZ. This generation – I don't get them. They don't even want to sing.

SHOO. Next to blinking, my favorite thing to do. There were always family sing-alongs.

BUZZ. Remember, when we first met? "Our" song?

SHOO. Course I do.

(Snuggles closer.)

BUZZ. *(Holds her and croons.)* "Shine little glow worm, glimmer glimmer

*(**SHOO** joins in.)*

Lead us lest too far we wander

Love's sweet voice is calling yonder – "

LUNY & MOONY. *(Yonder, calling, and rushing in, jumping about.)* Mom! Dad! Guess what?

BUZZ & SHOO. *(Startled. Quickly move apart, but still a bit woozy.)* What? What? What?

MOONY. We're going on tour!

SHOO & BUZZ. What! You're going on tour?

MOONY. Yes!! See – we met these really cool crickets –

LUNY. And they want us to join their group! They're a local band, and –

BUZZ. A band?

MOONY. It's a new rock group. They play at all the big rocks –

LUNY. And they want us to do their lighting –

MOONY. They been looking all over for some really cool lighting for their concerts.

LUNY. And we were exactly what they were looking for.

MOONY. They said we could help with the singing too.

LUNY. Flash publicity signs – for their big gigs.

SHOO. But, what about mating, starting families?

LUNY. Oh, we decided we wanted to wait. Plenty of time for that later. I don't want to be tied down, right now.

MOONY. We're just not ready yet – for family responsibility. There's too much we want to experience before settling down.

BUZZ. But, hanging out with those screechy crickets! We've told you to always stick with your own kind!

SHOO. We've never associated with crickets, or other lower species.

MOONY. World's changing, mom and dad. Integration, it's just happening all over!

LUNY. Everybody mixes, mingles now. It's soo cool, and colorful, and kinda wildlike.

MOONY. And those crickets, they're not screechy. They have the neatest sound. Captures the air waves and rides on your soul. They're looking at a recording deal too!

LUNY. There's even grasshoppers in their group. Nice long legged, quick hopping grasshoppers! With big hypnotic eyes. Blink, blink.

MOONY. They play the fiddle with their legs, thump drum leaves with their feelers –

LUNY. And know what they told us? That the greatest touring group ever, was – The Beetles!

BUZZ. The Beetles?

MOONY. Yes!! They got to fly all over the world. *(beat)* But – we're only fireflies.

SHOO. Welll, we never told you, but I guess it's time. *(beat)* You're not really flies.

MOONY. Huh? We're *not* flies? But, I thought –

BUZZ. No, you're really beetles! Because we have double wings, flies only have two. The family name for fireflies is really Lampyridae, some endomologist –

MOONY. This is so cool! Being a beetle! Maybe that's why joining this group appealed to us so much. Flies only buzz. But beetles can make all kinds of sonorous sounds, and we never knew it. We'll have to try them all! This is a most revealing night.

LUNY. The group has a dragon fly manager. And The Crickets are already booked –

SHOO. Already booked?

MOONY. Yep! We're going to play at the next Firefly Fest!

LUNY. We know you won't be around next Fest – to hear us.

MOONY. But, we just wanted you to know, we'll be okay.

LUNY. Don't wait up for us. This will be an all night session. A moonlight jamboree!

BUZZ. But –

SHOO. Let them go.

LUNY & MOONY. Bye mom and dad. Have a good retirement!

(Leave singing "Shake, Rattle, and Glow! Shake, Rattle and Glow!")

SHOO. They have a right to their own life. But, to hang out with crickets.

BUZZ. And use up all their light. Just for flickering rock shows.

SHOO. How will they find a mate?

BUZZ. Who will continue our traditions?

SHOO. Well, we can continue – what we started before.

(Both cuddle and begin gyrations.)

BUZZ. I guess I can get the lights going – one more time.

SHOO & BUZZ FLY.

(The singing gets slower and slower.)

"Shine little glow worm, glimmer glimmer

Hey, there don't get dimmer dimmer –

Light the path below, above – And lead us onto love – "

(Their lights slowly dim, and blinking lights go out one by one and stage is dark. Loud sound of Crickets is heard, then in the distance, in fast repeated voices. "Come on, let's – Shake, Rattle and Glow – Shake, Rattle and Glow"!)

The End

PRODUCTION NOTES

COSTUMES
– Greenish, glittery or reflective double wings, that possibly move.
– Headbands with antennaes.
– Fireflies should be dressed in dark colors from head to toe, except for accessories, which can be bright, showy.
– Use anything else to make these "special" fireflies.
– Give them firefly motions, expressions, maybe even their own little sounds.
– Make them magical and bright – zany and offbeat.

OTHER
– Set Background: At beginning, tiny greenish lights blink about the stage, possibly strands of Christmas tree lights hung in random display.
– Firefly family needs very small flashlights that blink on and off.
– A huge loglike structure, for family to sit or perch on, would be great stage addition, but not necessary.
– A woodlike setting would be ideal, but not necessary.
– Maybe crickets, cicadas, or other woodsy night sounds.
– Check out tune for "Glow Worm" song.
– Whatever can be added to enhance the script.
– Use your imagination! This is an imaginative story!

THE BEACH CLUB
(A Play in One Act)

The world premiere of **THE BEACH CLUB** was at the Village Church Theatre, Milwaukee, Wisconsin in October 1972. The cast was as follows:

JAKE..Tom Garvey
ALLEGRA...Pat Burtak
SIGMUND..Bill Martin
GRACE..Lovella Petersen

Director - Floyd Smith
Production Coordinator - Bob Gillo
Sound - Chuck Entrekin
Lights - Harvey Petersen

CHARACTERS

(in order of appearance)

WILMA – Older
JAKE – Early 60s. Slightly overweight
SIGMUND – Elderly. Trim body
GRACE – Middleaged
ALLEGRA – Late teens.

(***TIME:*** *December first*)

(***PLACE:*** *A beach, somewhere on the Great Lakes*)

(***SETTING:*** *Barren stage*)

(*Across the back, portions of a weatherbeaten wall remain. Everything is brightly lit, as if bathed in sunshine.*)

(***AT RISE:*** *Continuous sound of waves breaking.*)

(*Intermittent gusts of wind. Lone cries of gulls. A momentary feeling of emptiness.*)

(*Scene opens:*)

(*Sound of seagulls and continuous waves.* **WILMA,** *a strange looking creature, shuffles in from left, wearing long dark shabby coat, dark stockings and overly large slippers. Hair is gray and stringy. Carries a bent stick, using it as a prober/diviner rod. Hums tuneless little ditty in raspy tones. Exits right.*)

(**JAKE** *plods in from left, huffing, carrying arm loads of equipment and portable radio. Wears poplin coat, cotton print hat. Stands testing direction of wind, angle of sun. Picks spot right. Radio plays catchy gospel rock tune as he lays things out methodically.*)

(**JAKE** *gets into rhythm as he sets up his wooden canvas chair, the old-fashioned kind with canvas sling back. Ritualistically takes off coat, sweater, shirt, pants, shoes and socks. He is left wearing only colorful boxer bathing trunks and print hat. Stretches – a short form exercise, settles his well-tanned body into wobbly chair. Puts on sunglasses, gets our paper.*)

(**SIGMUND**, *gray hair, loose sweatshirt and pants, tennis shoes, jogs across from stage left.*)

SIGMUND. Good morning, Jake.

JAKE. *(His voice is overly loud, result of years at beach trying to be heard above the sound of the waves.)* Sigmund, old man. You still running round? Thought you gave up with all the rest of the softies.

SIGMUND. Just passing through, my good fellow. Just passing through....

(Exits right.)

JAKE. Well, stop by later, chew the fat some.

RADIO. *(Music fades.)* Annnd now, the latest weather report.

(**JAKE** *puts head close to radio.*)

Temperatures dropping before noon. Annd snow flurries expected with those lowering temperatures. So, get those snow shovels oiled up.

JAKE. Yowee! Today's the day. Knew those looked like snowclouds.

(A big beach ball bounces in.)

Hey, you kids, go on play somewheres else. This here spot's taken. Go on. Git.

(Gives ball fierce kick.)

Here she comes, plowing through that sand like a heifer cow.

(**GRACE** *enters left, plodding along slowly, carrying blankets and shopping bags. Dressed for winter.*)

JAKE. *(Claps hands.)* Grace, Grace – I see your face.

GRACE. Knock it off, Jake.

(Sets up things against back wall for shelter.)

JAKE. Dry cleaning plant keep you after school today, huh? Two minutes late, you know.

GRACE. Keep outa my life, will you.

JAKE. You keep out of this place then.

GRACE. You don't own this beach.

JAKE. Well, I got squatters rights on this here spot. I'm the first one down here every day –

GRACE. Can it. All I'm looking for is some fresh air after eight hours in that damn cleaning plant. I don't need more hot air from someone like you. Sitting on your rump here all day long.

JAKE. Hey, I put in my time. All those years at the pencil factory. I earned my rest. *(pause)* Did you hear it's going to snow today?

GRACE. Snow?

JAKE. Yep. Don't your astrology books predict the weather too?

GRACE. Sure, and winning lottery numbers, and –

JAKE. *(mocking)* Come on, Grace, what are my predictions for December? Big things going to happen?

GRACE. You wouldn't believe me if I told you. Never believe anything anybody tells you.

JAKE. I believe some. Wanta know why? Gypsy, she predicted my ma's death. Time. Place. Everything. Happened just like that gypsy said.

GRACE. You told me all that already.

(Picks up plastic pail.)

JAKE. – My ma, she jumped off that very bridge...Helluva thing for a kid to see. Body thrashing through the sky. Her, screaming like a banshee.

GRACE. Sorry, can't hang around to hear the rest. Going shell picking.

JAKE. Better pick those shells now, cause once that snow falls –

GRACE. *(Walks about, looking in sand for special shells.)* Well, you enjoy it while you can too, Jake, cause might be our last season down here.

JAKE. Who sez?

GRACE. Agnes, my landlady, told me they're planning to close up all the beaches next summer.

JAKE. Yeah, I heard that story before too. Just for swimming though. Cause water's all filled with gunk and stuff.

GRACE. Nope. She said the whole area would be fenced off. No one allowed here at all.

JAKE. Well, nobody's gonna keep me away from this place, by god. This here's public property.

GRACE. Just telling you what she said. Her Charlie, he shovels dirt in the county parks, so she thinks she knows everything what goes on at City Hall.

JAKE. *(Up in agitation. Takes off sunglasses, waving them around.)* Aagh, they'd probably do it too. Those bastards at City Hall. Sit on their asses all day long, behind a big fancy desk. In air conditioned offices. Then, then, they take their air conditioned cars to their air conditioned houses. Never get out into the real world –

GRACE. Just telling you.

JAKE. Hell, they don't wanta come down here, compete with the Mr. Americas. No siree, go to their private country clubs, where everybody else has a fat belly too.

(WILMA enters right.)

God, here she comes again. Why the hell don't they lock her up.

GRACE. Because some people don't need locking up. Good morning, Wilma.

(WILMA continues probing in sand. Walking in a large circle.)

JAKE. What the hell's she poking around with that stick for again?

GRACE. She told me once, when she still talked some, that she was a diviner.

JAKE. What the hell's a diviner?

GRACE. Special people, who use a stick, generally a willow branch – to search for water.

JAKE. Search for water. Proves she's wacky. Don't need to search for water down here.

(WILMA probes near JAKE.)

Go on, get outa here. Told you before to keep away from this place.

(WILMA gives JAKE a stare, then gives out a strange bird cry, between a crow and gull. Walks away.)

JAKE. Weirdo.

(A beach ball bounces in. JAKE quick jumps off his chair.)

Hey, you kids, I told you before to keep that ball out of here. *(Gives ball a fierce kick.)*

(GRACE gets up from sand, weaves a bit, puts hand to head and quickly grabs onto JAKE's chair, sitting momentarily.)

JAKE. Hey, get outa my chair.

GRACE. Feeling a bit dizzy – cleaning plant fumes –

JAKE. Well, sit on your blanket then. Told you before, no one sits in my chair. You want a chair to sit in, haul one down here by yourself.

GRACE. You are the most selfish person –

JAKE. That chair breaks, you gonna fix it? They don't make those kind no more.

GRACE. I wasn't breaking your chair. If your two tons don't break it – Just forget it. I'll look for my shells in a friendlier place.

(Takes pail and walks off, left.)

JAKE. Okay by me.

(Calling after.)

I'll look after your stuff. *(aside)* As usual.

RADIO. Here's another little joke to cheer up your day. Did you hear the one about the tightwad who figured out how to save money on his honeymoon? He went on it alone.

JAKE. *(Laughs boisterously.)* That guy cracks me up. Every time.

*(Radio fades into wave sounds as **JAKE** reads.)*

*(**ALLEGRA** enters quietly from behind fence. Wearing jeans and light blue sweatshirt. Her long hair flows in the breeze. Eyes focused downward. Each step is slow, precise, as if walking in slow motion. She clutches a bouquet of white flowers with ribbon streamers, with 'Rest in Peace' in gold printing.)*

*(The cry of the gulls is louder. Wind and waves more intense. **ALLEGRA** pauses stage left, an ethereal air about her as she looks out over the water. Slowly she plucks petals off the flowers, scattering them into the wind. Sounds fade, as she begins singing softly, like the cry of a wounded bird.*

*(**JAKE** looks up from his reading. Listens quizzically.)*

ALLEGRA. "Oh, he's gone away – He's gone away –
For to stay a little while
But he's coming back....

(Breaks off, stifling a cry. Continues.)

Oh who will tie your shoes?
And who will glove your hands?
And who will kiss your ruby lips?

(almost a whisper)

When I am gone...."

(She stops. Waves thunder as she throws remaining bouquet toward water. Clutches arms tightly around herself as if warding off a sudden chill. Then lifts face toward the sun as waves quiet.)

JAKE. Nice little song, Allegra.

ALLEGRA. *(Speaks with slight Southern accent.)* Jake! I'm sorry– I didn't even see you there.

(Finds spot far stage left, near front. Spreads soft sand-colored blanket. Sits hugging knees, staring out, absently letting sand sift through fingers.)

JAKE. Haven't seen you round for awhile

ALLEGRA. I've been here. Sometimes at night. Sometimes –

JAKE. Not a good idea. Coming down here at night, young girl, all alone –

ALLEGRA. All alone....

JAKE. Where's the boy today?

ALLEGRA. What?

JAKE. Your little guy – you always bring him.

ALLEGRA. Jonathon? He's – he's not with me....

JAKE. Be pretty cold down here for him today anyways. You hear the weather report? Predict snow.

ALLEGRA. *(vaguely)* Snow?

JAKE. Yep. Before noon too, they say.

ALLEGRA. I've never seen snow....

JAKE. You're kidding. Never seen snow?

ALLEGRA. Down South, where we lived – it never snowed.

JAKE. I'll be damned.

ALLEGRA. *(Addresses **JAKE**, but as if she were speaking through a separating glass wall.)* Jonathon and I only moved here last May.... Everything was blossoming. Beginning new life....

JAKE. December first. Snow time round here.

ALLEGRA. When I was a child, my favorite fairy tale was *The Snow Queen*. As I read it, I would imagine the whole world transformed into glistening white....

JAKE. *(Stands. Looks out over water.)* Just look at those clouds. Moving in pretty fast.

ALLEGRA. Are those snow clouds?

JAKE. Yep, that's them all right.

ALLEGRA. But, they're so dark. I always thought snow clouds were white, pure white.

JAKE. Nah, they're gray. Just like rain clouds.

ALLEGRA. *(introspective)* How mystifying. Those dark, ugly clouds – they're going to give birth to tiny bits of snow.

JAKE. First snow's quite a thrill, I tell you.

ALLEGRA. Something new and fresh and clean entering the world once more...Nothing ever continues in its original form, does it. And everything that's born, dies...

JAKE. Snow don't die. Just melts away.

ALLEGRA. I always thought snow poured forth from fluffy white clouds.

(introspective) In kindergarten, that's how I drew my pictures. A huge white cloud in the corner, and snow showering from it, like feathers from a pillow.

(Looking out. In a reverie.)

– And my trees were always full of the greenest leaves.
– And the water – gentle waves of brightest blue.
– And the sunshine – sprays of scattered gold.
– And the grass, once I colored it, stayed green forever.
– And the people in my pictures, were permanent too.
– Never changed, never grew old. And, nothing ever died....

(Back to reality.)

That was – when I was in kindergarten.

(Sits on blanket.)

JAKE. *(Begins working crossword puzzle in paper.)* I hated kindergarten. Hated every day of school.

ALLEGRA. *(happier mood)* Jonathon, he kept asking me about the snow. Because I told him, when we moved up north, we'd see snow everywhere.

(Rises.)

And I'd picture to him what a fairyland the world would be. Everything sparkling like diamonds.

JAKE. Yeah, does change things a bit.

ALLEGRA. And I promised him we'd go sledding. Build snow men.

(Sits staring ahead, slowly letting sand sift through fingers)

JAKE. Abbreviation for building –

ALLEGRA. *(Tears forming.)* Every day, he'd keep asking, *When's the snow coming, Mama? Is today the day?* And I'd always say, *Tomorrow, Jonathon. Tomorrow the snow will come*.... Tomorrows never arrive, do they.

JAKE. Aagh, this puzzle's too dang hard today.

(Closes paper.)

You ain't too cold are you?

*(**ALLEGRA** doesn't answer.)*

I mean, you don't have no extra padding like me.

(Pause. Talks, but to no one in particular.)

You know, I must have bear instincts, cause when I see that first snow, smell it in the air even, I get this feeling inside me, to go hibernate in my room. I got this big old fur rug – curl up under it most of the day...Sometimes, I just lay there and eat peanuts. Buy a hundred pounds in fall. Shells all over the damn place. But, why bother. Wish I really was a bear, sleep the whole winter through.

ALLEGRA. It would be nice to sleep away parts of our life we don't want to live through. Erase them all with sleep.

(Takes out bottle of pills. Stares at it.)

JAKE. Hate winters. Always have. Aagh, when I was a kid, my ma, she'd bundle me up so, could hardly walk. Long underwear, wool socks, snow pants. Scarves all over my face. Couldn't even see. And those smelly flannel rags, dipped in hot rancid goose grease, pinned to my undershirt. Itched like hell. Vicks up my nose, pine and tar cough syrup down my throat. All winter long, couldn't breathe.

*(Stops as he notices **ALLEGRA** taking pills from bottle and swallowing them.)*

What's that you're taking there, Allegra?

ALLEGRA. Pills.

JAKE. Pills? You ain't one of them addicts, are you?

ALLEGRA. *(without emotion)* No....

JAKE. Didn't think so. Nice girl like you. What you taking pills for anyways?

ALLEGRA. Pain.

JAKE. Oh.

(Back to his rambling.)

I'd be careful bout taking too many pills. 'Cept for my heart, don't take any. I'm afraid of pills. My ma, she used to stuff me with them. Pills for this, pills for that. Had some to ward off the devil even. Worst were those laxative pills. Shoved them down me regularly. Along with the bran and molasses cookies. Embarrassing as hell at school. And the kids, they knew, too. Sometimes, they held the door to the stall shut – and I couldn't get in – and I couldn't wait –

(pause)

Then one time, when I was in the hospital, after my accident at the pencil factory, they gave me some shiny blue pills. Saw all kinds of strange things. Scared the hell out of me. Room started moving. Monsters all over the place. Kept telling myself it was only a nightmare. But, I knew damn well I was awake.

ALLEGRA. You said – you saw things?

JAKE. Sure as hell did.

ALLEGRA. Do you ever have visions?

JAKE. Visions? What do you mean?

ALLEGRA. Can you ever see things that happened before?

JAKE. Well, on TV you can. Instant replay. See everything just exactly like it was before.

ALLEGRA. It happens to me sometimes. Especially when I come down here.

JAKE. What happens?

ALLEGRA. I see everything that went on here before. All the people – It's like they never left.

JAKE. Those cream puffs leave all right. First cold day, take off like jackrabbits.

ALLEGRA. But they come back?

JAKE. Maybe. Next spring.

ALLEGRA. They come back. Because we always return to places where we were happy, don't we?

(Takes small book of poetry from purse.)

JAKE. Some come back. Not all. Beach Club changes every summer.

ALLEGRA. I came back. Because I was happy here – once.

JAKE. Gonna do some studying?

ALLEGRA. Thought I might read some poems. *(pause)* Would you like me to read you one?

JAKE. Nah. Don't understand that poetry stuff.

ALLEGRA. This one – this one's very special. Would you like to hear it, Jake? No one else here today.

JAKE. Okay. Read one, just one.

ALLEGRA. *(rises)*

"The visions fade though we strive to hold
For dreamland's shore is a shifting sand.
Is life the thing that our youth foretold?
I speak no answers for words are cold;
I only stretch out my hand.…"

*(Looks to **JAKE** for reaction.)*

JAKE. That it?

ALLEGRA. *(repeats)*

"I only stretch out my hand.…"

(Stretches out her hand. Then covers mouth to stifle a cry. Sits.)

JAKE. Sorry if I didn't understand your poem.

ALLEGRA. I don't understand it either. I don't understand anything today.

JAKE. Well, you just go read your little book. I'm gonna get me some exercise.

*(Takes out badminton racket and bird. Draws two circles in sand with toe. Tries to hit bird into alternate circles. Taking his time. **ALLEGRA** sits staring ahead.)*

Hey, you think your friend will ever show up again?

ALLEGRA. My friend?

JAKE. Yeah, you know – Mr. America?

ALLEGRA. *(not understanding)* Mr.?

JAKE. That handsome boy friend of yours. We nicknamed him 'Mr. America.'

ALLEGRA. Brady?

JAKE. Yeah. That guy in the white sports car. Think he'll ever show up again?

ALLEGRA. I don't know....

JAKE. Two seasons, comes down here, every day. Never said a word to nobody. Oiled himself up. Lay in the sun. Then shoots away in his white sports car. Till you came along.

ALLEGRA. He said he'd be back. Some day.

JAKE. Those kind don't come back. He's gone, honey. Gone like the wind. Probably went to Florida for the winter. Most of those boys do, you know. Keep up their tan.

ALLEGRA. *(to herself)* Jonathon and I, we waited and waited.

JAKE. *(Continues bouncing bird, not really listening to **ALLEGRA**.)* Yep, probably gone to Florida. Looking for a rich girl. Don't know why he came down here, to a public beach. Huh, no rich people down here, that's for sure.

ALLEGRA. They're both – gone.

JAKE. Aagh. I sure wouldn't lose no sleep over that guy. Young girl like you – can always find another.

(Pauses in playing, leaning on racket. Reminiscing to himself.)

You know, I used to drive a sportscar. Bright shiny red one. Always filled with pretty girls. Lots of em. Had a real firm body then too. Before the accident, the heart trouble.

(Gives bird fierce whack. Goes to retrieve it. Lighting dims somewhat.)

Clouds sure moving in fast.

(Sits. Takes out detective magazine.)

(Space Odyssey-type music comes in faintly. Continues in background during following sequence.)

ALLEGRA. *(Looking out.)* Look! It's happening again. All the people – they're coming back.

(Stands. Trembling.)

They're gathering together. Moving into focus. The beach – it's crowded once more. So terribly crowded.

JAKE. *(Looks around.)* Ain't nobody here, Allegra.

ALLEGRA. They're moving about now. In slow motion. Almost as if they're dancing....

JAKE. *(puzzled)* Nobody here, but us.

ALLEGRA. I can see them. Feel them all around me.

JAKE. *(still puzzled)* Kind of a haze over the lake right now. Makes things look a bit fuzzy.

ALLEGRA. *(Moves about freely, as if in a dream.)* It's summer time again. And, it's warm, so very warm.

JAKE. I've sat here in fog so thick sometimes. Thought I saw people too, but –

ALLEGRA. *(Joyously, as lights brighten.)* Look! The sun's shining! And – and – all the people are back.

JAKE. *(A final statement.)* It's empty, Allegra. Empty as hell.

ALLEGRA. Oh, I see some one. Excuse me, I have to go find him.

(Runs off right.)

JAKE. What the heck's the matter with her today?

(Gets out cards and begins playing solitaire on folded magazine. **SIGMUND** *jogs in from left.)*

Hear the weather report, Sigmund? Have to give up your jogging once that snow hits.

SIGMUND. Snow? No. Just slows me down some. Makes the tennies a bit soggy.

(Stops near center. Takes off sweat top and does series of calisthenics. Push ups, side bends, head stands, with ease and expertise.)

JAKE. Well, if the snow don't stop you, cold sure will.

SIGMUND. Sure won't. I used to belong to the Polar Bear Club even, way back.

JAKE. Aagh, those guys, bunch of exhibitionists. I mean, big splash once a year, for coupla minutes. Everybody watching. Photographers around. So, they jump into Lake Michigan on New Year's Day. Big deal.

SIGMUND. It isn't all that easy, believe me.

JAKE. Aagh, anybody can do something once. Do it. Get it over with. But, when you do something, day after day – that's a whole different ball game. I mean, like coming down here, no matter what the weather. That takes real guts.

SIGMUND. You think so?

JAKE. I know so. I been doing it.

SIGMUND. Why? What's so important about it?

JAKE. Well –

SIGMUND. You probably don't know yourself. People, as they grow older, keep doing things just out of habit.

JAKE. It's not any habit. It's just – something – I gotta prove to myself.

SIGMUND. So, what does it prove?

JAKE. *(Stops playing cards and makes the next statement as if it summed up his whole philosophy of life.)* Well, you gotta do something, so you're remembered. Leave some mark in this world. I mean, there's gotta be something you do better'n anybody else....

SIGMUND. And you think you'll be remembered for sitting on the beach.

JAKE. Probably.

(Back to playing Solitaire.)

SIGMUND. So, who's going to remember you for sitting on the beach?

JAKE. Well, you ain't been coming round here long enough to know all about me. But, oh, back bout six years, this newspaper photographer, he comes down here, wants to write me up.

SIGMUND. That right.

JAKE. But, I'm no publicity seeker. Not like them Polar Bear Clubbers. Certain people to know I come here. So, I said, Okay, write me up. But no name, no picture of my face. So, they printed this big story, front page, bout the mystery man on the beach, who comes here first day of spring, stays till the first snow of winter.

SIGMUND. That right.

JAKE. Lots of people come round that year. I got clippings to prove it. Then, the radio guy, Fritz the Bummer, he even came down once to interview me. So, there's plenty of people who'll remember me.

SIGMUND. People go look at monkeys in the zoo, too.

JAKE. *(Gets so upset, knocks over magazines and cards.)* Look! I don't have to take that kind of crap from nobody. I was only trying to give you a serious answer. But seems you're the only one allowed to talk serious round here.

SIGMUND. Sorry my good fellow. I didn't mean –

JAKE. *(Gets up, picking up cards.)* Nobody asks you to stop here, you know.

SIGMUND. Awfully touchy today, aren't you.

JAKE. *(Putting cards away.)* Well, I don't like being compared to monkeys in the zoo.

SIGMUND. I wasn't comparing. Just meant, people will gather to watch anything.

JAKE. Damn right they will.

(Sits in chair again. Gets out toe nail clippers, begins clipping toe nails.)

My dad, he was a flag pole sitter.

SIGMUND. He was?

JAKE. Yep. Sat on top that flag pole for thirty one days. Nights too. Now that was really something to see. Crowds of people standing below, just waiting for him to give up. My ma, she stood there every day too, madder'n a wet hen, screaming at him to come down. Didn't pay no attention to her. Just sat there. Waiting out his thirty one days.

Now there was a man what could endure things. Hell, sitting down here is nothing compared to him spending thirty one days on top that tiny flagpole...Lots of times, gets pretty nippy down here, I think – what the hell am I proving anyways. Then, I start thinking bout my dad, sitting up there, never giving up. And you know what he said to me day he came down? He said, "Son, it was worth every minute of it. I finally did something spectacular in my life, and nobody can ever take it away from me!" Even on his deathbed, asked to see the clippings. And there was a smile on his face when he went, like his life wasn't wasted after all.

SIGMUND. Yes, people do strange things to get attention.

JAKE. Attention! You think he did it for attention? Aagh, you wouldn't understand. You didn't know my dad.

SIGMUND. *(Relaxes from exercises.)* No, but I knew my father. Not when he was living. After he died, that's when I finally got to know him.

JAKE. *(laughs.)* Can't know people after they die.

SIGMUND. *(rises)* He was a preacher, a traveling evangelist. Waved his hands. Stamped his feet. Anything to get attention.

JAKE. Heh heh – son of a preacher.

SIGMUND. No clippings when he died. Only a worn out finger-thin bible. But, there's people who still remember his words. And, every once in awhile they come back to me, like I was hearing my father's voice all over again.

(Begins jogging in place.)

JAKE. Yeah, well maybe he'd tell you that jogging's not good for your heart.

(Takes out bag of popcorn, munching and eating. **SIGMUND** *goes back to his calisthenics.)*

I got a heart condition you know.

SIGMUND. I think you told me.

JAKE. Don't usually like to talk about it. But that's why I don't exercise. I mean, well, I'd rather stay alive than be thin.

SIGMUND. Sure. Sure.

JAKE. Hell, I used to be able to do all those, more too. Before the accident. Heart trouble.

SIGMUND. The heart. Always the heart. What's good for the heart? A genuine case of love. Only time you should worry about your heart.

JAKE. Easy for you to make fun. But, I go to bed every night never knowing if I'll wake up in the morning or not.

SIGMUND. Do any of us know?

JAKE. Always gotta have the last word, don't you.

SIGMUND. Each of us has only one last word, Jake.

(Pulls top on and starts exiting left.)

Well, I better be on my way. Five more laps to go.

JAKE. So, who's gonna know if you cheat a little.

SIGMUND. I would. I keep the records for myself.

JAKE. *(Shouting after.)* Yeah well, when you do something spectacular, like sitting on a flagpole, then somebody else keeps the records.

(Finishes popcorn. Throws bag away.)

ALLEGRA. *(Enters right without **JAKE** noticing. Runs toward Center. Slows, relieved.)*

There he is. There's Jonathon. Playing in the sand – with his pail and shovel.

(concerned) Oh dear, he's much too close to the water. Those huge waves – they're washing his sand castle away. They could carry him away too. He's so small.

(calls) Jonathon!

JAKE. *(loudly)* You didn't bring the boy today, Allegra. He's not here.

(Sits. Takes out detective magazine.)

ALLEGRA. *(To* **JAKE**, *but almost as if he were a stranger.)* I'm sorry. I didn't mean to disturb you. But, my little boy, he was too near the water, and this giant wave was coming –

(Turns away, more frightened.)

I've got to bring him back. Where he's safe. He shouldn't be alone.

(calls) Jonathon!

(Waves thunder as **ALLEGRA** *starts walking toward the water.* **JAKE** *shakes his head and goes back to reading.* **ALLEGRA** *walks back, with hand out, as if holding a smaller person's hand. Waves quiet.)*

ALLEGRA. *(in gentle scolding tones)* I've told you to keep away from the water. You must stay near Mommy. Always.

(happier mood) Come, let's build another sand castle. Away from the water. We'll build it together. Okay?

(Kneels in sand stage left, begins building imaginary sand castle. Laughing and giggling in process.)

Look how big it's getting, Jonathon. Let's build the biggest castle we've ever built. And, we won't knock this one down. We'll save it for Brady to see. Okay? Look Jonathon! How it glistens in the sunlight. Like millions of tiny diamonds piled one atop another. Castle's almost taller than you, Jonathon.

(Stops. Looks out.)

Look. There's Brady!

(Stands up.)

Brady's come to visit us. Maybe he'll help us build our castle. He's smiling, Jonathon. He's walking toward us. Now, he's laughing. Let's call to him. Come on. "Brady!"

(Laughs joyously. Pause.)

He doesn't hear us. Let's call louder – "Brady!"

(Almost screaming.)

Brady! He's turning away. He's leaving.

(Calls out frantically.)

Brady! Here we are! Over here! By the sand castle..... He's disappearing.

(Kicks at castle. Punches it down fiercely.)

He probably couldn't see us behind this castle. Stupid castle!

(Space Odyssey-music begins. She looks about frightened.)

The other people – they're leaving too. They're all going away. And the sun – it's getting dark again.

(Lights dim somewhat. Calling frantically.)

You don't have to leave – just because the sun's fading. You don't have to disappear too!

(Looks about wildly, then calls out.)

Jonathon! Where did you go? Come back, Jonathon! Don't go near the water – there's a big wave coming!

(Screams hysterically.)

Jonathon! Jonathon!!!

(Complete silence.)

JAKE. What's the matter, Allegra?

ALLEGRA. *(Terrified agonized cry.)* Jonathon.

(softly) Jonathon – he's gone....

JAKE. Why were you screaming like that?

ALLEGRA. *(puzzled and dazed)* I don't know. I – I thought I saw Jonathon....

(Sits down. Takes more pills.)

JAKE. Didn't know what was happening to you. Sceaming your head off. Like you was having a nightmare or something. My wife used to have nightmares. Scared the hell out of me. Had to slap her awake. Couldn't stand her screaming like that.... You okay?

ALLEGRA. *(Walks over to* **JAKE.** *Little girl quality to her voice.)* Mama, my dolly, Rosalinda, and I are going to sit quietly on the porch steps here. We won't bother you at all.

(Sits near **JAKE.**)

JAKE. You sure are acting kooky today.

(Back to reading.)

ALLEGRA. Look at the clouds, Rosalinda. There's a horse! There's a camel! And there's a beautiful lady in a long pretty dress...Mama, when I grow up, I'm going to wear long pretty dresses and sprinkle flowers in my hair. And dance in the wind, and –

(pause)

Am I grown up now, Mama? Is this how being grown up feels? Thousands of knives going through you, all at once.

(Breaks into uncontrollable sobbing.)

JAKE. Quiet down there, girl. No way to act in public.

ALLEGRA. I can't stop.

JAKE. *(stands)* Look, we don't like crazies down here. Why don't you just go on home.

ALLEGRA. I want to go home, so badly, but –

JAKE. *(Tries to lift her to her feet.)* You better take your things then, and go on get outa here now.

ALLEGRA. *(Rises. Backs away. Looking at* **JAKE,** *in terrified scream.)* Mr. Gorski! No! Keep away. Don't touch me!

JAKE. *(Shaking her shoulders.)* What the hell's the matter with you.

ALLEGRA. *(Screaming out.)* Mama! Mr. Gorski's after me again. He's trying to –

JAKE. *(Shaking her harder.)* You just quiet down there. My name's not Gorski.

ALLEGRA. Keep away from me! You can't do that!

JAKE. You want the whole place to hear you!

ALLEGRA. *(Screams out.)* No! No!

JAKE. I told you to shut up.

(Unable to control himself, he slaps her. Backs off, realizing what he's done.)

ALLEGRA. *(Sinks into sand, sobbing. Wraps blanket tightly around herself.)* Mama…Mama.…

JAKE. I wasn't going to hurt you. I'm not that kind. I just didn't want you screaming anymore.

(Turns and walks away.)

ALLEGRA. *(Calls from under the blanket.)* Help me. Somebody help me.…

JAKE. You help yourself, girl. I tried. Nobody's gonna accuse me of stuff like that. Not today anyways.

(Sits in chair and tries to read, but still agitated.)

GRACE. *(Trudges in from behind fence.)* Well, that's my shell picking for the season.

JAKE. I'm trying to read, so don't bother me.

GRACE. Suits me fine.

(Sits. Puts on glasses for reading.)

Say, who's that under the blanket? Sophie come down while I was gone?

JAKE. No. That's Allegra.

GRACE. Allegra? Why, she hasn't been here since –

JAKE. Well, she's here now. And, she's sleeping. So don't disturb her.

GRACE. Sleeping? So, where's the boy?

JAKE. Didn't bring him.

GRACE. She always brings him.

JAKE. Well, today she didn't.

GRACE. I wonder –

JAKE. Said she just wanted to be left alone. That's all people ask – to be left alone.

GRACE. Probably didn't want to listen to you anymore. Neither do I. So, I'm going to read and eat in peace.

(Reads and eats sandwich. **WILMA** *wanders in from behind fence and stands in front of* **GRACE.**)

JAKE. Well, that moocher ain't gonna let you eat in peace.

GRACE. Here you are, Wilma.

(WILMA snatches bread and begins tearing it into bits, throwing them toward water, making croaking birdlike sounds.)

JAKE. *(Getting more agitated.)* Go on – get away. Throw your bread some place else. We don't want birds here all the time. Dropping their dirt.

(WILMA lets out strange bird cry. Waves her stick, almost as a farewell to the birds, and walks away.)

JAKE. Women sure turn into strange creatures.

(Beach ball bounces in. JAKE gets up and grabs it.)

I told you kids to keep that ball away from here. This time you ain't getting it back.

GRACE. Give them back their ball, Jake.

JAKE. Nobody's getting this ball back. Ever!

(Picks up his nail clippers.)

GRACE. Give them their ball back.

JAKE. *(Snips ball, deflating it, then stomps on it.)* All right – they can have their ball –

(Throws limp ball.)

Here! Here's your ball!

GRACE. You mean, miserable S.O.B.

JAKE. Well, if their parents don't teach them, somebody has to.

(Goes to his radio, tuning it loudly in frustration.)

GRACE. Turn that damn radio down!

JAKE. You don't tell me what to do.

SIGMUND. *(Jogs in from left.)* Hey, I thought this was a place of peace and quiet.

GRACE. Not when he's around.

JAKE. You don't like it, keep away.

SIGMUND. It is rather loud, Jake.

JAKE. Well, okay.

(Turns it down.)

For you. Cause you ask for things nicely.

SIGMUND. Thank you.

(Jogs in place.)

Is that Allegra under the blanket? I saw her wandering the beach before, like she was in a daze.

JAKE. Just tired, that's all.

GRACE. I don't think she's warm enough.

JAKE. Told you, she's okay.

GRACE. Well, I don't need this old blanket anymore. Just put it over her. Save me dragging it home.

JAKE. Always got to stick your nose in where –

GRACE. If someone needs help, yes.

(Walking over. Kicks at sand. Pauses. Picks up few petals, examines them.)

What's all this white stuff on the ground?

JAKE. Flower petals. Had some white flowers when she came down. Picked off the petals. Threw them around. Don't know why. Strange girl.

GRACE. Looked like snow at first. They've blown on top of her too. She's covered –

JAKE. *(Breaking in, singing.)* "Covered all over – with sweet violets!"

SIGMUND. *(joining in)* "Sweeter than all the roses – "

JAKE & SIGMUND. *(heads together)*

"Covered all over from head to toe –
Covered all over with –"

GRACE. Hey. I thought I felt a bit of snow.

JAKE. *(Singing stops. Suddenly animated.)* Snow! By god, it's come. December first and it's here already. Last year, was December tenth.

GRACE. Not enough yet to run around shouting about.

SIGMUND. *(Looks up solemnly.)* The first snow of the season. A magnificent event.

JAKE. *(Walks about excitedly.)* Coupla hours. By the time the photographers come round, ground will be all covered. Today's the day, Fritz!

GRACE. Well, I'm not sticking around for any photographers.

(Starts packing.)

Finish my lunch and reading at home. Next to that new portable heater.

JAKE. You gonna hang around?

SIGMUND. I haven't decided yet.

JAKE. Well, if the photographers come, best if I'm here alone.

SIGMUND. What difference –

JAKE. Well, you see, I'm supposed to be the last guy on the beach, and –

SIGMUND. I understand.

GRACE. Flakes are really coming down now. I better wake Allegra.

JAKE. She's okay, I told you.

GRACE. Well, I'm not just going to leave her sleeping down here, not when it's snowing.

*(Goes to **ALLEGRA**. Let's out a cry.)*

Oh, my god.

SIGMUND. What's the matter?

(Rushes over. Pace quickens from here on.)

GRACE. Child's cold as ice.

JAKE. *(Still seated. Still placid.)* Said she was warm enough.

SIGMUND. *(Touching her.)* Cold right through.

GRACE. Still breathing, thank God.

SIGMUND. Pulse is low –

GRACE. We've got to get her warm, fast.

*(**ALLEGRA** moans incoherently.)*

Allegra, what's the matter?

ALLEGRA. Jonathon...

GRACE. Sounds delirious.

JAKE. Talking in her sleep, that's all. My wife –

GRACE. Will you just shut up for once! We've got to get her home. Some place. Know where she lives?

JAKE. *(Miffed because he's been told to shut up.)* Nope. Never asked.

GRACE. *(to SIGMUND)* Look in her purse. See if there's an address, phone number.

JAKE. That's private property –

GRACE. Nobody asked you.

SIGMUND. Empty pill bottle.

JAKE. Yeah, she was taking some pills before.

GRACE. What kind? How many?

JAKE. I don't know. Whole lot of them.

GRACE. We better get her to a hospital, just in case.

JAKE. Hospital? What for? Don't believe in hospitals.

GRACE. Will you stop your mouthing, and – go flag down a car.

JAKE. Can't. My heart – can't go fast up those stairs.

GRACE. Damn you and your lousy heart.

(to SIGMUND)

Keep her warm and sitting up. I'll go get help. Won't hurt my heart at all.

(Exits.)

JAKE. Grace knows bout my heart. Knows I can't go fast.

SIGMUND. *(holding ALLEGRA)* Such a fragile soul. Such pale skin.

JAKE. Don't question why women take pills.

SIGMUND. She's starting to shake.

JAKE. Acted funny before too.

SIGMUND. My dog, when he was dying, all I could do was hold him. Let him know I was near. Sometimes, that's all we can do for another's pain – just let them know we are near.

(Strokes her hair gently. She continues moaning, "Jonathon.")

There, there....You'll be all right.

ALLEGRA. Help me....

SIGMUND. We're getting help. Wish Grace would hurry.

JAKE. Grace is faster with her mouth than her feet. I told Allegra before not to stay down here. Just hope she don't cause more problems.

SIGMUND. *(Picks up poetry book. Opens cover.)* "To Allegra, my soulmate – Brady."

JAKE. *(laughs mockingly)* Allegra – his soulmate. So, he gave that book to her, huh.

SIGMUND. "Tonight you give me roses

And kiss me a last adieu;

Tomorrow they all will wither

And I shall be gone from you –

But as long as the world has roses,

As long as love shall be –

I shall think of tonight forever

And all that you are to me...."

GRACE. *(Returns hurriedly, huffing and angry.)* Not one of them would stop. Screamed myself hoarse.

JAKE. You could be a dangerous character, you know.

GRACE. Park office is closed for the season too.

SIGMUND. Her breathing's not good.

GRACE. We better carry her to the top ourselves. See if we can flag down some car on Lake Street. Or call an ambulance – or something.

(Starts wrapping **ALLEGRA.***)*

We'll need help carrying her up all those steps. Come on Jake, help us.

JAKE. Well, I – I – I don't want to get near her.

GRACE. It's nothing contagious, you fool.

JAKE. *(Stands.)* Well, before, when I tried to help her, she started screaming.

(Sits down.)

GRACE. Stop your jabbering and get over here.

JAKE. Can't.

GRACE. Why? Why can't you?

JAKE. Because – my back, my bad back. Too much strain for it.

GRACE. Girl's dying and you're worried about yourself as usual.

JAKE. She's not dying. You women get all excited over nothing.

GRACE. You go ahead then, flag down a car. That won't hurt your back.

JAKE. I can't.

SIGMUND. Come on, Jake. You can come back down. Still be here for the photographers.

JAKE. *(firmly)* No. I'm not leaving this spot.

(Begins fiddling with radio. Loud blaring music comes in.)

GRACE. *(Rushes over, grabs radio, forcefully throws it into sand.)* Damn you and your asshole radio.

JAKE. *(Furious, grabs **GRACE** and begins shaking her.)* What the hell you doing, woman!

GRACE. Keep your hands off me, you bastard!

JAKE. (**GRACE** *frightens him off. He goes to pick up radio. Close to tears.)* Broke. You broke my radio. Now what am I going to do?

GRACE. Who the hell cares!

JAKE. Who's gonna pay for this?

(screaming) Who's gonna buy me another radio?

SIGMUND. Calm down, man. Just calm down. Allegra needs quiet.

*(**JAKE** sits in chair, carressing the radio.)*

GRACE. Leave him be. This child's more important right now.

SIGMUND. Up we go.

GRACE. Be gentle with her.

*(**ALLEGRA** stirs.)*

SIGMUND. It's all right dear. We're taking you for help.

ALLEGRA. *(Reaching out. Thrashing arms.)* Jonathon! Come back!

(One last scream, then goes limp.)

GRACE. Oh god, she's passed out.

SIGMUND. We better hurry.

*(**GRACE** grabs most of her things, leaving pail of shells. They slowly begin to carry **ALLEGRA** off. They manage, but are obviously overloaded.)*

JAKE. *(Still shaking his radio. Looking up as they pass.)* See, you didn't need me anyways.

GRACE. Nobody needs you, Jake. Nobody at all.

*(Poetry book drops from **ALLEGRA**'s things.)*

JAKE. Hey, you dropped something.

(They ignore him. He turns front. Self pity.)

They don't understand. Wife didn't either. Something happens to me, nobody's going to take care of me. I got nobody.

(Shudders as if chill suddenly overtook him. Pulls towel around shoulders. Tries to psyche himself into cheerful mood.)

Hell, photographers might have come while I was gone. Then what? Helluva thing – First snow of winter and King of the Beach is missing.

(pause)

Aagh, she probably wasn't dying anyway. They get all excited over nothing. Specially that Grace.

*(**WILMA** wanders in humming. Sees poetry book. Pokes at it with stick.)*

Hey, leave that alone. Don't belong to you.

*(**WILMA** ignores him, doing ritualistic dance around book, jabbing at pages with her stick.)*

I told you to get away.

*(Grabs her stick and breaks it in two, throws pieces to left. **WILMA** screams unearthly sob, grabs broken pieces and crouches/crawls off like a wounded animal, emitting pitiful whimpers.)*

JAKE. And don't come back here again. *Ever.*

(Sits in his chair. Agitated silence. Sits up suddenly. Peers out.)

I'll be damned. Looks like a white sports car.

(Takes out field glasses. Puzzled.)

Hard to see with the snow. But recognize that body anywhere.

(Puts glasses down. Smiling.)

You're too late, Mr. America. Way too late.

(Sits back smugly. Arms folded.)

Look for her you son of a bitch. Look for her all you want. She ain't here. And she ain't coming back.

(Peers through field glasses.)

Huh. Snow's melting on his face.

(Mocking.)

Looks just like tears. Big fat tears rolling down his pink rosy cheeks.

(pause)

Sitting down now, on that big gray rock. Just sitting there. Gotta be him. Posing. Staring this way.

(Glasses down. More to himself.)

She ain't coming back, Mr. America. They carried her away. No use hanging around here anymore.

(Stands up. Shouts.)

You can leave, Mr. America. Your soulmate gave up waiting for you.

(Picks up poetry book, waving it.)

See this! All what's left. Your book of junky poems. Didn't even want them no more. Threw them away.

(Opens book. Mockingly.)

"To Allegra, My soulmate –"

(Begins laughing.)

JAKE. Joke's on you, Mr. America. Because she took some pills. Whole bottle of pills and she won't be back.

(louder and more ugly)

Go on! Climb into your fancy sports car and go look for somebody else.

(Pause. Intensity building within. Explodes in frantic screams.)

SHE'S DEAD, MR. AMERICA! ALLEGRA'S DEAD. GO ON, GET OUT OF HERE. NOBODY'S LEFT HERE BUT ME. I'M THE LAST ONE DOWN HERE. THE BEACH IS CLOSED!

(Hysterically waving book as he shouts.)

NO ONE ELSE IS ALLOWED DOWN HERE AFTER THE FIRST SNOW. THIS IS MY BEACH. AND YOU CAN'T STAY HERE. GET OUT. GET OUT OF HERE, YOU SON OF A BITCH!

(He starts to throw book at Mr. America, then stops, clutching his heart. Book falls to sand. He finds it hard to catch his breath. He huffs and puffs, but still continues shouting.)

THERE'S NOBODY HERE! NOBODY. I'M THE LAST ONE DOWN HERE!

(still struggling)

I survived them all. Every damn one of them. Froze my ass off every day – and what did you do? Nothing but show off your damn filthy body…

(Grabs onto chair as he begins collapsing into sand.)

Help me! Somebody help me!

*(Chair folds up on him as he falls, capturing him in agonizing position. He's trapped, can't move. Tries to

shout, but his voice is only weak gasps, which become continuously weaker as lights grow dimmer.)

Help me! Mr. America! Please – help me – !

(Collapses completely)

I can't see him – nothing anymore. Snow's too thick.

(Struggles to get up. New fear in his voice.)

In a few hours – I'll be buried. They'll never find me.

(A last rally.)

The photographers, they'll find me.... Every year, first snow, they come to take my picture. Last survivor on the beach.

(pause)

They better hurry. I don't know – how much – longer – I can wait – for them. Hurry! Hurry, damn you. Find me. Save me!

(His eyes close. Mouth drops open in grotesque position. Reaches out his hand in one last effort. It falls grasping toward opened poetry book.)

*(Spot on **JAKE** narrows. Cry of gulls begins faintly. Wind and wave sounds rise in crescendo, as stage slowly darkens.)*

*(Spotlight becomes swirling gray snow as **ALLEGRA**'s voice echoes ethereally.)*

ALLEGRA. "Is life the thing that our youth foretold –
I speak no answers for words are cold,
I only stretch out my hand.... I only stretch out my hand...."

The End

PRODUCTION NOTES

WILMA

Wears long dark shabby coat. Dark stockings and overly large slippers.
Carries stick used as diviner wand

JAKE

Wears poplin coat, sweater and shirt. Print hat. Colorful boxer bathing trunks.
Carries in portable radio.
In bag:
- Sunglasses
- Newspaper
- Detective magazine
- Badminton racket and bird
- Deck of cards
- Toenail clippers
- Small bag of popcorn
- Fieldglasses

SIGMUND

Wears loose gray sweatshirt and pants, white tennis shoes.

GRACE

Dressed for winter. Coat, head scarf, etc.
Carries in blanket.
In bag:
- Plastic pail
- Reading glasses
- Sandwich
- Magazines

ALLEGRA

Wears jeans and light blue sweatshirt.
(If preferred, could wear a long loose gown.)
Carries:
- Sand colored blanket
- Bouquet of white flowers with ribbon streamer "Rest in Peace"
- Small purse with bottle of pills, small book of poetry

SHELTER SKELTER
(A Play in Ten Minutes)

The world premiere of **SHELTER SKELTER** was held November 13, 1992, at the Village Playhouse of Wauwatosa. The cast was as follows:

DESK CLERK..Evvie Smith
APPLICANT...Marion Ziemienski
WOMAN...Phyllis Ruck

CHARACTERS

(in order of appearance)

CLARENCE – Desk clerk. Harried, with pretentious officiousness. (can also be played as "Clarita," a female)

ANNIE – Middle-aged woman. Poor, down and out, but dignity still there.

MRS. SINCLAIR – Older lady. Elegantly dressed. Decidedly upper crust.

(*SETTING:* Plain room. *"ANIMAL SHELTER"* sign on wall. High counter-type desk. A few waiting chairs. Animal noises – dogs barking, cats, birds screeching.)

(*AT RISE:* Animal sounds fade. **CLARENCE** is on phone. **ANNIE**, carrying shopping bag full of personal items and rolled up blanket. Keeps banging desk bell.)

CLARENCE. I'm sorry I cannot give you that information by phone. You'll have to come down in person. Yes, in person…Thank you.

(*Bangs phone down. Phone rings.*)

Sidney Shelton Animal Shelter…No, I'm sorry we do not accept animals that size. We just do not have the room, the capacity…Well, try the zoo then…THE ZOO!…No sir, I do not know who can help you!

(*Slams phone down. To* **ANNIE**, *who's still banging bell.*)

Please!

ANNIE. (*Hands him papers.*) Here, here you are sir. All filled out.

CLARENCE. Let's see – Annie Penkalski. That your dog's name?

ANNIE. Nope. My name.

CLARENCE. Well, what kind of animal are you applying to put in, or take out of the shelter? This information you put down is very sketchy.

ANNIE. The application's for me, dummy. I'm the one who wants shelter!

CLARENCE. You!

ANNIE. Yeah, me. I need a roof over my head more than any of these dumb animals.

CLARENCE. There must be some misunderstanding.

(*Officious and precisely.*)

This is an animal shelter!

ANNIE. *(repeating his rhythm)* Sooo – I am an animal.

CLARENCE. So, we don't accept "human" animals.

ANNIE. I don't care, animal is animal, and this one needs shelter.

CLARENCE. Look lady, there's lots of places specially set aside where people like you can stay.

ANNIE. No, there ain't –

CLARENCE. Have you tried?

ANNIE. You bet your booty. Lots of times…. Like zoos. Crazy people all over the place. I'm better off in the streets. Only today – weather's getting so blistery cold, and –

(**MRS. SINCLAIR** *enters carrying large animal cage. Looks bit perturbed that someone is ahead of her. Sits in chair, twiddling thumbs and looking skyward.*)

CLARENCE. *(noting new arrival)* Lady, this is a very busy day here. I do have other people to take care of.

ANNIE. Don't brush me off! I filled out all the forms, like you said. Answered each and every question, like you said.

CLARENCE. Well, I didn't know it was for yourself.

ANNIE. I said I needed shelter. You said "fill out the forms" and shoved them at me.

CLARENCE. These forms are only for stray, homeless animals.

ANNIE. Which I am.

CLARENCE. Sorry. Next.

(**MRS. SINCLAIR** *rises and sits.*)

ANNIE. Wait a minute Buster, you ain't through with me yet.

CLARENCE. I most certainly am. The door opens out. Next.

(**MRS. SINCLAIR** *rises and sits.*)

ANNIE. Not fit weather out there, for one of your dogs even. You can't turn me away – into that killer storm.

CLARENCE. What would you like me to do?

ANNIE. All I'm asking for is a place to stay.

CLARENCE. There is no place! Not here! This shelter only has cages!

ANNIE. Well, I wouldn't mind a cage. Not if I could have one by myself. Those other places, never by myself. Always some other riff raff around. Jails? Now those are cages.

CLARENCE. Well, you cannot stay here. Can't you read? See, the sign, "Animal Shelter"! A- N- I-

ANNIE. I can read. And I can see too. I can see you got a super duper snazzy place here. Rich people – they give lots of money to this la-di-da shelter. Those other "people shelters," only the government gives them money. And government money gets siphoned off into so many grasping hands. Shelters must be at the bottom of their list. The pits. The real pits!

CLARENCE. Well, here is not possible. All our food is served in metal dishes, and –

ANNIE. No problem. Right now I don't eat out of anything.

CLARENCE. There no beds, and –

ANNIE. Beds? Hey, I been sleeping on sidewalks. Talk about hard. Newspapers been my only mattress. Rocks for pillows.

CLARENCE. Lady, I think you might have a few – mental problems. We are not equipped to help disturbed people.

ANNIE. I am not disturbed! Well, yes I am. About the way I have to live. Eat. But I'm smart. I figure things out. And I figured out I could very well cope with living in an animal shelter.

CLARENCE. But –

ANNIE. And, if you cleaned me up real nice, and I was bright and smiling and better fed – Maybe someone might even adopt me.

CLARENCE. This is ridiculous!

ANNIE. And maybe then I might get to go to a good home, where I'd be fed every day. And I wouldn't have to work. Just roam around the big house. And, they wouldn't even have to clean up after me. I take care of myself.

CLARENCE. But –

(*MRS. SINCLAIR has been half dozing, begins to listen.*)

ANNIE. I sure wouldn't mind sleeping on a big soft fur rug. I wouldn't even mind a chain around my neck, when they walked me. But, I'd never run away. Not if I was treated okay. And I wouldn't bark, or smell, or bite small kids. I'd make a very good pet. Honest.

CLARENCE. I'm sorry, but –

ANNIE. And I'd be good at protecting from burglars too. I can spot one real easy. The good ones, the bad ones.

MRS. SINCLAIR. (*up to desk quickly*) Excuse me, I couldn't help hearing this conversation. You see, we had to put Shep to sleep just last week. Old age. So, I came here today hoping to adopt a special animal to possibly replace Shep. And I was hoping it wouldn't be just an ordinary animal, because Shep was not just an ordinary dog –

CLARENCE. I'll be right with you, Mrs. Sinclair, soon as I finish –

MRS. SINCLAIR. (*rings bell again*) You don't understand, I'd like to adopt this "animal," this one here, applying for shelter. It sounds just like what I might be looking for…I had been thinking about a hairless animal. Shep shed so much hair.

CLARENCE. But –

MRS. SINCLAIR. How do I go about it? It's just that I'm all alone in this big house. I need a pet – a companion. Something.

ANNIE. Huh? Would you – could you adopt me?

MRS. SINCLAIR. Oh yes, I think it could work out very well.

ANNIE. I'd be a very good house pet. I learn rules real quick, and –

MRS. SINCLAIR. Well, I wouldn't cook your meals for you. Of course I wouldn't give you dog food – though we do have so much left over from Shep. Maybe just probably a bowl of milk and some dry cereal?

ANNIE. Sounds good to me. *(Smacks lips.)*

MRS. SINCLAIR. And I'd like your hair to grow long – longer, so I could pet it. I loved petting Shep's beautiful fine hair.

ANNIE. Oh, I love to be petted. Can't remember the last time anyone even touched me.

MRS. SINCLAIR. You could sleep at the foot of my bed, to keep my feet warm at night, like Shep did. It's a very big bed.

ANNIE. Oh, I could do all that. And I could learn tricks too. Fetch the paper. Bring your slippers. Sit up. Beg. I'm good at begging.

MRS. SINCLAIR. And when I go walking I wouldn't have to carry that awful pooper scooper.

ANNIE. I love to walk. Some days I walk miles before I find any food. Mostly in garbage cans.

MRS. SINCLAIR. Well – I really wouldn't want you using our bathroom. The maid only comes in once a week now – Yet, I don't suppose you can bathroom outside like Shep did. He even had his own little door to go in and out…Hmm. Well, there is an old drain hole in the basement. We'll work something out I'm sure.

ANNIE. And you'll give me baths?

MRS. SINCLAIR. We'll give you everything. Clothes. Shep had lots of sweaters. Nail trims. You're going to be such a well cared for animal.

ANNIE. That's all I want. All I'm really asking for – to be cared for. Nobody before ever really cared for me.

MRS. SINCLAIR. I have always given my pets extra special care.

ANNIE. It's like a wish – a dream – come true. I can't believe this is happening. Wake me up somebody. No, don't. Please don't!

CLARENCE. *(mutters)* Nobody told me there'd be days like this.

MRS. SINCLAIR. All right then, let's have those adoption papers.

CLARENCE. But –

MRS. SINCLAIR. Look, I'm a very big donor to this place, and –

CLARENCE. Yes, I know. Here.

(Hands papers to her.)

MRS. SINCLAIR. Now Sheppie – No, I think I'll call you Pootsie. You look like a little loveable old Pootsie. Cutesy, Pootsie.

*(Carresses **ANNIE**'s face and hair.)*

You just stay here like a good little doggie, while mama fills out your papers.

ANNIE. *(Begins to bark and whine in a cajoling manner.)*

MRS. SINCLAIR. That's enough! Now just quiet down till I'm through. I hate filling out papers for pets, they can never help me with the answers.

ANNIE. I can help. I can read.

MRS. SINCLAIR. Wonderful! I just knew I picked the right pet.

CLARENCE. *(Retrieves papers quickly and tears them up.)* I'll just tear these papers up right now, and you can take her – it, without papers. Only on this one, there is no return. No nothing! We will not be responsible for any diseases, bad behavior. No papers. No shots. It's only between the two of you. The Shelter is absolved.

MRS. SINCLAIR. Good! Then no owner can come to claim her.

*(**ANNIE** starts trying to get into cage.)*

No, no Pootsie – not the cage, we're gong to go home in a cab!

*(to **CLARENCE**)*

Here, you can keep this cage. A tax deduction donation.

ANNIE. *(Jumps up on* **MRS. SINCLAIR**.*)* A cab! A real cab! Oh, I'm going to be treated even better than a dog.

MRS. SINCLAIR. Of course you are. I even brought Sheppie's jeweled collar along. Hmmm. Won't fit around your neck. Well, we'll just strap it onto your wrist then.

(Puts jeweled dog collar around **ANNIE***'s wrist.)*

There now, when I jerk this leash, you stop. Okay? Oh, there's so much I have to teach you.

ANNIE. I'll learn. I'll learn. WOOF! WOOF!

MRS. SINCLAIR. Treats, every time you do a good trick. Now, come along, Pootsie. Good doggie.

(They exit grandly, as **CLARENCE** *stares after. Phone rings.)*

CLARENCE. *(Answers phone in monotone voice.)* Sidney Shelton Animal Shelter.

(Goes into super fast verbal rampage.)

This is an Animal Shelter – can't you understand! An animal shelter! I cannot help it if you got the wrong number. It is not my problem if you get the wrong number, the wrong place. I'm where I should be. I'm in the right place. It's all those other people – I didn't want to deal with people! That's why I took this job. Animals don't think – Talk back –

(Continues ranting as lights dim and distant animal sounds come up drowning out **CLARENCE***'s voice.)*

The End

PRODUCTION NOTES

CLARENCE – Offbeat clothing.
ANNIE – Dowdy but neat clothing. Maybe a battered hat she takes on and off. Carries overflowing beat-up shopping bag.
MRS. SINCLAIR – Elegant upper crust attire. Maybe excessive jewelry.

ONSTAGE
- Counter type desk.
- Forms on desk to fill out.
- Desk bell
- Phone (preferably cradle phone).
- Waiting chairs.
- Large sign "ANIMAL SHELTER."

OFFSTAGE
- Large animal cage.
- Jeweled dog collar (to fit human wrist).

See what people are saying about
SAVING AMERICA & OTHER PLAYS...

"Ludmilla Bollow's *Saving America* succeeds as ironic satire, pushing the general discomfort with the aged and aging process to the point of savage extreme...Bollow does so with passion, economy, and rich inventiveness."
- Alan Woods, Professor, Ohio State University,
and coordinator of the Heckart Drama Contest

"Playwright Ludmilla Bollow has found a speedy way of condensing the evolutionary social process of a culture passing on its traditions and beliefs to the coming generations. She uses fireflies. In *Flickering Fireflies*, Bollow presents a simple, funny, and poignant metaphor for the moment when children break with their parents and the parents are left with the "what next" moment."
– Prof. Woodrow Hood, Drama Judge for
Wisconsin Council for Writers

"*The Beach Club* is an engaging play...Fascinating look at peculiarities of diverse characters and their interaction with each other"
– The Shoestring Theatre, Victoria, Australia

"In *The Beach Club*, based on a true story, Jake finds meaning in life through his determination to sit on the beach from the first day of Spring till the first snow of Winter no matter who or what must be sacrificed."
– *TSI Playtime Series*, New York

"The crisis of the homeless is given a touching treatment in Ludmilla Bollow's *Shelter Skelter* in which a street person successfully finds succor at an animal shelter"
– Jay Joslyn, *Milwaukee Sentinel*

"*Shelter Skelter* had a wicked premise and biting performance by the cast of three talented women."
– David M. Doll, Marquette Theatre Festival

OTHER TITLES AVAILABLE FROM SAMUEL FRENCH

IN THE REST ROOM AT ROSENBLOOMS

Ludmilla Bollow

Comedy / 4f and 9 extras (can be doubled) / Interior

This contemporary comedy reveals the hopes, dreams and fears of three elderly ladies who spark their lonely lives by meeting daily in the rest room lounge of an outdated downtown department store, and the crazy/touching events that occur the day one of them is supposedly threatened. There's Myrah, with a fighting spirit that totters into the absurd; Violet, a leftover from the days of elegance; and Winifred, a wisp of a woman who wanders in and out of reality. A steady stream of bizarre events occur as the ladies seek to protect Winifred from being taken away by her sister Clare, leading to a blockade of the rest room and a final triumph over those who would threaten their fragile freedom. Winner of the Southeastern Theatre Conference New Play Award.

"The women are wonderful characters...[the play does] an excellent job of balancing humor against the basically pathetic lives of the three main characters."
– *Minneapolis Tribune*

"A very funny play of character and situations. You can't get much better than that writing-wise: check out William Shakespeare..."
– *Appleton Post Crescent*

"Visit to Rosenblooms is worth the trip. Quirky characters, punchy lines and light hearted humor."
– *Driftwood News*, Canada

"Hilarious one minute and surpisingly touching the next."
– Gallery Theatre, California

"Maybe the best comedy is the one that makes you cry. This Ludmilla Bollow script is an almost perfect example of the classic dramatic unities of time and place."
– *Neenah Post Crescent*

"It's comedy, but has very poignant moments in it as well."
– *Go-Erie.com*

SAMUELFRENCH.COM

OTHER TITLES AVAILABLE FROM SAMUEL FRENCH

THE MAN IN THE GRAY SUIT & OTHER PLAYS

Lisa Soland

Various m and f roles

From the author of *Cabo San Lucas, Waiting,* and *Truth be Told,* comes six new one act plays about love and relationship. Perfect for any theatre. Included in this book are: *The Man in the Grey Suit, Different, Red Roses, The Same Thing, Knots,* and *Come to the Garden.* All have simple casting and production requirements, all are easy to stage.

"Ms. Soland has developed several plays...all interesting, all clever, all unique. She is gorgeously talented."
– Charles Nelson Reilly.

"Soland's work is so audience friendly...she has an uncanny ear for dialogue."
– *Los Angeles Times*

"If you are looking at this book as a possible source of performance material, you are in for some work. Lisa Soland doesn't cut any slack to the actors and directors. Her work is demanding. Be prepared to sweat, curse and spend many frustrated nights staying awake, searching for that extra level you just know she's put there. Yes, hard work. But it's the kind of hard work that leads to the intense joy of success. With subjects as diverse as answering the question 'What is the purpose of Art?' or finding the common ground between a couple separated by a huge personal loss, Lisa manages to find a simple and easy way to make those topics, and the characters involved, accessible to the audience. Yet her simplest works have more layers and meanings than the vast majority of complicated works being shown in major houses. I wholeheartedly recommend this book and these plays. Read on and enjoy."
– Steven L. Sears (writer/producer)

SAMUELFRENCH.COM